Affirm,

Visualize, and

Achieve

A 30 Day Journey to a New You

Casondra R Wilson

ISBN-13: 978−1542665766

DEDICATION

This journal is dedicated to my father, Robert J. Wilson, Sr. I will always be forever grateful for the support he had for his children. No matter what, we always knew that daddy had our back. In hind-sight, I see that not only was he our supporter in the present things, but the future things as well. Even when we didn't know our own potential, daddy did. I didn't fully see that before he passed away, so now I want to take the time to say thank you.

With Love,

Your baby girl

Presented

To:_____

From:_____

God's Intention for Our Lives

Through out the bible, it mentions much about God's intent for us. One of my favorite passages says, "For I know the plans that I have for you . . . plans to prosper and not to harm you, plans to give you hope and a future", Jeremiah 29:11. (ESV).

God wants nothing but the best for his children. One of his greatest desires is for us to be able to see things the way he intended for our lives. In order for us to become a catalyst for change in our personal lives; we must be able to see the modifications in the making and then put some action behind it!

Putting actual work into this journal will allow you to make things happen. Prayerfully in 30 days you will see your words change into action. That being said, let's go activate!.

Preface

By dictionary definition. to "affirm" something, , means to declare something to be true.   An affirmation is usually a sentence or phrase that is repeated regularly to make a formal declaration of your intention; your say and do comes together. . While some may say it is akin to "fake it until you make it," I see it a bit more like holding true to the vision of what I know can be true.

When you say an affirmation over and over again, a couple of things happen.   The 1st thing is that a very clear message is sent to your brain to specify the personal attachment (IE: this is important to me). The 2nd thing is, you are displaying the belief that it is not only possible but probable- "positive visualization".   You can see it coming to pass and it shall!.   In essence, the affirmation starts to move you towards the truth of what you know instead of just something you're lay your hope.

Many of us have heard that it takes 21 days of repetition to change or create a habit.   It is the same for positive affirmation.   You have to first say it, then see it and once you see it in reach the sky is the limit! So we're going to purpose for no less than 30 days.   In the beginning it will take some getting used to, but around day 22 watch out!   I can just imagine what you will create; there is no limit!

Affirmations of Gratitude

Day 1:

Today I am grateful for life and all that I experience within it!   I overcome, I grow, and I prosper at times.

Psalm 51:10

[10] Create in me a clean heart, O God; and renew a right spirit within me.

Action Steps:

Today I will (I did) do the following to move toward my goal:

_____

_____

Reflection:

_____

_____

_____

Day 2:

Today I feel an abundance of gratitude for everything I have and receive every day. My needs and desires are generously met. For this I am thankful.

Philippians 4:19

[19] And my God shall supply every need of yours according to his riches in glory in Christ Jesus.

Action Steps:

Today I will (I did) do the following to move toward my goal:

_____

_____

Reflection:

_____

_____

_____

Day 3:

Today I clearly see the beauty of life that flourishes around me.   I give gratitude for God's endless treasures.

I Thessalonians 5:18

[18] give thanks in all circumstances; for this is the will of God in Christ Jesus for you.

Action Steps:

Today I will (I did) do the following to move toward my goal:

_____

_____

Reflection:

_____

_____

_____

_____

Day 4

Today I am grateful for my ancestors living on through my blood; my cup is running over.   I am grateful to be allowed to represent those who came before me in this space and time.

Psalms 31:19

[19] Oh, how abundant is your goodness, which you have stored up for those who fear you and worked for those who take refuge in you, in the sight of the children of mankind!

Action Steps:

Today I will (I did) do the following to move toward my goal:

_____

_____

Reflection:

_____

_____

_____

Day 5:

I am continually amazed at how abundant my life is already! I appreciate everything I have and I show my sincerest gratitude to those that I love.

I Corinthians 13: 8, 12

[8] Love never ends. As for prophecies, they will pass away; as for tongues, they will cease; as for knowledge, it will pass away. [12]For now we see in a mirror dimly, but then face to face. Now I know in part; then I shall know fully, even as I have been fully known.

Action Steps:

Today I will (I did) do the following to move toward my goal:

_____

_____

Reflection:

_____

_____

_____

Day 6:

Today the universe pours joy into my life.   It has my cup
overflowing with wealth, health, and love.

Luke 6:38

[38] give, and it shall be given unto you; good measure, pressed down,
shaken together, running over, shall they give into your bosom. For
with what measure ye mete it shall be measured to you again.

Action Steps:

Today I will (I did) do the following to move toward my goal:

_____

_____

Reflection:

_____

_____

_____

Day 7:

Today I clearly see the beauty of life that flourishes around me.   I give gratitude for God's endless treasures and for that I am most grateful.

Eccleasiastes 3:11

[11] He has made everything beautiful in its time. Also, he has put eternity into man's heart, yet so that he cannot find out what God has done from the beginning to the end.

Action Steps:

Today I will (I did) do the following to move toward my goal:

_____

_____

Reflection:

_____

_____

_____

Day 8:

I am grateful for all the great health, love, and goodness that my life has revealed to me.   My life is Godly unique and wondrous. For this I am profoundly thankful.

Psalms 107:1

[1] Oh give thanks to the LORD, for he is good,for his steadfast love endures forever!

Action Steps:

Today I will (I did) do the following to move toward my goal:

_____

_____

Reflection:

_____

_____

_____

Day 9:

I am grateful to have a beautiful life filled with happiness and love. I am rewarded with all the joy life can offer.

Colossians 3:23-24

[23] Whatever you do, work heartily, as for the Lord and not for men, [24] knowing that from the Lord you will receive the inheritance as your reward. You are serving the Lord Christ.

Action Steps:

Today I will (I did) do the following to move toward my goal:

_____

_____

Reflection:

_____

_____

_____

Day 10:

I am so grateful for every person and everything in my life. I am grateful for my blessed ancestors living on through my blood.

Hebrews 12:28

[28] Why we receiving a kingdom which cannot be moved, let us have grace, whereby we may serve God acceptably with reverence and godly fear.

Action Steps:

Today I will (I did) do the following to move toward my goal:

_____

_____

Reflection:

_____

_____

_____

Day 11:

I naturally attract great things in my life, speaking my vision loudly and proud, creating word in action!

Mark 11:23-24

[23]Truly, I say to you, whoever says to this mountain, 'Be taken up and thrown into the sea, and does not doubt in his heart, but believes that what he says will come to pass, it will be done for him. [24]Therefore I tell you, whatever you ask in prayer, believe that you have received[a] it, and it will be yours.

Action Steps:

Today I will (I did) do the following to move toward my goal:

_____

_____

Reflection:

_____

_____

_____

Affirmations of Confidence

Day 12:

I am confident, I am strong and powerful. This day I will speak with boldness because I exude God-like confidence in the presence of all I connect with today.

Proverbs 3:26

26 for the LORD will be your confidence and will keep your foot from being caught.

Action Steps:

Today I will (I did) do the following to move toward my goal:

_____

_____

Reflection:

_____

_____

_____

Day 13:

Everyday my confidence is increasing.   I will boldly go after what I want in life.   I will always meet a difficult challenge with confident action.

Acts 28:31

[31] Proclaiming the kingdom of God and teaching about the Lord Jesus Christ with all boldness and without hindrance.

Action Steps:

Today I will (I did) do the following to move toward my goal:

_____

_____

Reflection:

_____

_____

_____

Day 14:

I will always meet a difficult challenge with confident action. Others look up to me as leader because of my confidence.

Romans 12:8-9

[8] if it is encouraging, let him encourage; if it is giving, let him give generously; if it is leading, let him lead with deligence; if it is showing mercy, let him do cheerfully. [9] Love must be sincere. Detest what is evil; cling to what is good....

Action Steps:

Today I will (I did) do the following to move toward my goal:

_____

_____

Reflection:

_____

_____

_____

Day 15

I will always believe in myself and my ability to succeed.   I confidently meet any challenge and I confidently speak my mind without hesitation.

Mark 9:23

[23] And Jesus said to him, " 'If you can'! All things are possible for one who believes."

Action Steps:

Today I will (I did) do the following to move toward my goal:

_____

_____

Reflection:

_____

_____

_____

Day 16:

I confidently meet opposition.   Every day I become more confident, powerful, and assertive.

Colossians 10:35-36

[35] Therefore do not throw away your confidence, which has a great reward.   [36] For you have need of endurance, so that when you have done the will of God you may receive what is promised

Action Steps:

Today I will (I did) do the following to move toward my goal:

_____

_____

Reflection:

_____

_____

_____

Day 17:

I am outgoing and confident in social situations.   I always stand up for myself and my beliefs.

Romans 12:2

[2] Do not be conformed to this world, but be transformed by the renewal of your mind, that by testing you may discern what is the will of God, what is good and acceptable and perfect.

Action Steps:

Today I will (I did) do the following to move toward my goal:

_____

_____

Reflection:

_____

_____

_____

_____

Day 18:

I am becoming more sure of myself with each passing day. I am starting to confidently assert my thoughts and opinions.

II Thessalonians 3:4

[4] And we have confidence in the Lord that you are doing and will continue to do what we command.

Action Steps:

Today I will (I did) do the following to move toward my goal:

_____

_____

Reflection:

_____

_____

_____

_____

Day 19

I whole-heartily believe in myself because until I do, no one else will. I have unbreakable confidence within myself.

Proverbs 14:26

[26] In the fear of the LORD one has strong confidence, and his children will have a refuge.

Action Steps:

Today I will (I did) do the following to move toward my goal:

_____

_____

Reflection:

_____

_____

_____

_____

Day 20

I am transforming into someone who always stands up for what they believe in!   Confidence come naturally to me.

II Corinthians 5:17

[17] Therefore, if anyone is in Christ, he is a new creation, The old has passed away; behold, the new has come.

Action Steps:

Today I will (I did) do the following to move toward my goal:

_____

_____

Reflection:

_____

_____

_____

_____

Affirmations of Personal Growth

Day 21

Today I am free from my past regrets. I am at peace. My mind is focused on enjoying the present moment.

John 8:36

[36]So if the Son sets you free, you will be free indeed.

Action Steps:

Today I will (I did) do the following to move toward my goal:

_____

_____

Reflection:

_____

_____

_____

Day 22

I am transforming into someone who is always learning, discovering, and developing. Everyday I recognize a different aspect about myself and I love it!

I Peter 2:2-3

[2]Like newborn infants , long for the pure spiritual milk, that by it you may grow up into salvation— [3]if indeed you have tasted that the Lord is good.

Action Steps:

Today I will (I did) do the following to move toward my goal:

_____

_____

Reflection:

_____

_____

_____

Day 23

I am consistently improving myself. I am always developing myself in every area of my life. I feel a deep sense of power and possibility within myself.

Joshua 1:9

[9] Have I not commanded you? Be strong and courageous. Do not be frightened, and do not be dismayed, for the Lord your God is with you wherever you go."

Action Steps:

Today I will (I did) do the following to move toward my goal:

_____

_____

Reflection:

_____

_____

_____

Day 24

I am a positive thinker.　Thinking positively is becoming easier and more natural.　I find it easy to maintain a positive attitude

Matthew 5:7

[7] Blessed are the　merciful, for they shall receive mercy.

Action Steps:

Today I will (I did) do the following to move toward my goal:

_____

_____

Reflection:

_____

_____

_____

_____

Day 25

I am focused on being the best I can be at all time.   I believe in myself deeply.   I naturally expect to succeed at whatever   I am doing.

Roman 8:24-25

[24] For in this hope we were saved. Now hope that is seen is not hope. For who hopes for what he sees? [25] But if we hope for what we do not see, we wait for it with patience.

Action Steps:

Today I will (I did)   do the following to move toward my goal:

_____

_____

Reflection:

_____

_____

_____

Day 26:

Today I see my personal growth as an important part of my walk with God.   I am changing daily and like my transformation more and more.

Ephesians 4:23-24

[23] Instead, let the Spirit renew your thoughts and attitudes. [24] Put on your new nature, created to be like God—truly righteous and holy.

Action Steps:

Today I will (I did) do the following to move toward my goal:

_____

_____

Reflection:

_____

_____

_____

_____

Day 27:

Today my mind is focused on excelling in every area of my life.   I am becoming an independent and powerful human being.

II Corinthians 4:16

[16] So we do not lose heart.   Though our outer self is wasting away, our inner self is being renewed day by day.

Action Steps:

Today I will (I did) do the following to move toward my goal:

_____

_____

Reflection:

_____

_____

_____

_____

Day 28:

I am always developing myself in every area of my life.   I feel a deep sense of power and possibility within myself.

II Timothy 1:7

[7] for God gave us a spirit not of fear but of power and love and self-control.

Action Steps:

Today I will (I did) do the following to move toward my goal:

_____

_____

Reflection:

_____

_____

_____

_____

Day 29:

Each day I find it easier to take action and go after the things that make me happy.   I will succeed because I am determined!

James 2:14, 17

[14] What good is it, my brothers if someone says he has faith but does not have works?   Can that faith save him?   [17]So also faith by itself, if it does not have works is dead.

Action Steps:

Today I will (I did) do the following to move toward my goal:

_____

_____

Reflection:

_____

_____

_____

Day 30:

Believing in myself is natural and normal. My mind is focused on excelling in every area of my life because success is who I am!

Ephesians 4:22-23

[22] to put off your old self, which belongs to your former manner of life and is corrupt through deceitful desires, [23] and to be renewed in the spirit of your minds.

Action Steps:

Today I will (I did) do the following to move toward my goal:

_____

_____

Reflection:

_____

_____

_____

Notes or Reflections

_____

_____

_____

_____

_____

_____

_____

_____

_____

_____

_____

www.ingramcontent.com/pod-product-compliance
Lightning Source LLC
Chambersburg PA
CBHW040316010626
45792CB00022B/590